How Do We Build A Real

WAKANDA?

Social analysis inspired by the major motion film Black Panther

Sean XLG Mitchell

EDITED VERSION OF SEVEN

How Do We Build A Real Wakanda?

By Sean XLG Mitchell

Published by:
ALB Management and Publishing Co.
A Division of Team XLG
Fort Washington, MD
albmngt@gmail.com / Seanxlg@gmail.com

M. Mitchell, Editorial Director
C. Mitchell, Associate Publisher
Chris Howard, Associate Editor
The Printed Page, Interior Design / Cover Layout

"To control a people you must first control what they think about themselves and how they regard their history and culture. And when your conqueror makes you ashamed of your culture and your history, he needs no prison walls and no chains to hold you."

– Dr. John Henrik Clarke

Contents

"The Civil Rights and Voting Rights Acts of 1965 made great strides toward racial equality. However, this legislation — ending decades of government-sponsored racial oppression and intended to reverse the effects of hundreds of years of slavery — by no means resolved racial inequality in the United States.

Racial differences in the United States are prevalent regardless of geography. While social and economic gaps are wider in some states than in others, the gaps exist across all areas, and we were unable to identify any states where black Americans are better off than white residents. For this reason, we expanded last year's list of the 10 worst states for black Americans to include all 50 states.

Across virtually all social and economic measures, there are wide racial disparities. Compared to white people in the United States, African Americans are considerably less likely to own their homes, twice as likely to be unemployed, nearly three times as likely to live in poverty, and five times more likely to go to prison".

- *Black and White Inequality in All 50 States* by Thomas C. Frohlich, Evan Comen and Michael B. Sauter
Published in August, 2016

<u>How Do We Build A Real Wakanda?</u>

How do we build a real Wakanda? Wakanda of course is the fictional city in Africa where the Black Panther comic book series and blockbuster movie is based. Let's be clear, there is no city in Africa by that name. In fact, it originates from a Native American term so when we ask *'how do we build a real Wakanda'* we are speaking in general terms as a metaphor in regards to the emergence of a new African centered paradigm.

Wakanda is presented as being steep in culture, history, and tradition. These are the aspects of every prominent nation around the globe. Aside from the fictional character of Black Panther with super powers and a high tech costume, the views and values of a people who carry themselves with dignity and respect is what we're are pointing to in this particular work.

In a sense, Wakanda is every city where its' people are united and working towards positive outcomes. The fact that we are referencing Africa and African people takes on a special meaning because the movie Black Panther symbolizes our triumphs and reflects our unlimited potential.   It is no secret that over the past 400 years we have suffered as a result of slavery, colonialism, segregation, racism and discrimination.

Now we must ask the question what is hope? What is faith, what is power? What is pride and determination? How do we stand on our own two feet? And if we were never subjected to the European invasion how far along would we be today without the cultural and social restraints that continue to linger beyond the Maafa?

Ultimately, how do we heal ourselves and the answer is to bring about a reality that was fictionalized in the city of Wakanda. In order to do so we must first build up the people because it is the people who build a nation.

<u>**A Cultural Orientation**</u>

Who are some of the most powerful and prominent races and ethnic groups of people in the world today? And our definition of power means; a people who are self-sufficient and sustaining in terms of social, political and economic wealth and stability, are formidable in regards to world power and influence, and are able to independently govern themselves. By all accounts, we are speaking of the people of China, Russia, Saudi Arabia, Israel and the United States. These are some of the power nations on the planet.

The United States, unlike the other countries mentioned, is vastly multi-cultural and comprises of a multitude of nationalities but for the sake of what we're presenting here we are referring specifically to White America because they represent the majority of the U.S. population and historically, the most dominant in terms of power-albeit ill gained (the institution of slavery). Nevertheless, from Washington, DC, and Wall Street to the corner store on Main Street, White America rose to an equal position to other powerful nations.

What are the keys to their success and how did they attain their elite positions in the world? There is no one-size-fits-all answer but the one thing they all have in common is a cultural orientation. Culture is the key to a people's empowerment. Culture empowers a people because it organically brings about a collective consciousness that unifies people which constitutes power. The primary elements of culture are language, education, religion, names and customs, a basic set of characteristics that are unique to each race and ethnic group of people.

The following are examples of the cultural elements of each country:

China:

- <u>Language</u>: Mandarin
- <u>Education</u>: Chinese; history and philosophy (dynasties of Shang, Ch'in, Han, Sui, T'ang, Ming and Qing, etc.), socialism and personalities
- <u>Religion</u>: Confucianism, Taoism, Buddhism
- <u>Common Names</u>: Zhang Wei, Wang Fang, Li Wei, Wang Xiu Ying, Li Xiu Ying, Li Na, etc.
- <u>Customs</u>: chop sticks, tea, rice, xun and guqin (instruments), martial arts, dragon dancing, celebration of the Chinese New Year, etc.

Russia:

- <u>Language</u>: Russian (East Slavic)
- <u>Education</u>: European and Russian history; East Slavs, Tsardom, Russian Empire, Oleg of Novgorod, Russian Revolution, communism, socialism, personalities, etc.
- <u>Religion</u>: Orthodox Christianity

- Common Names: Chernoff, Falin, Davidovich, Ivanov, Romanowski, Sliva, Polansky, etc.
- Customs: Ballet, borsch (soup), Vodka, Baba Yaga, Christmas on Jan. 7th, Russia Day Celebration, etc.

Israel:

- Language: Hebrew
- Education: European and Israeli history, Abraham, socialism, personalities, etc.
- Religion: Judaism
- Common Names: Pascal, Rothschild, Sheinberg, Meier, Hirsch, Krakowski, Horowitz, etc.
- Customs: Yom Kippur, Bar and Bat Mitzvah, Rosh Hashanah, Kosher foods, Passover, Mensch on a Bench, etc.

Saudi Arabia:

- Language: Arabic
- Education: Saudi Arabian history, Ummah, the Prophet Muhammad, Arab socialism, personalities, etc.
- Religion: Islam
- Common Names: Ali, Muhammad, Abdullah, Khan, Abdur-Raheim, Rahman, Jabbar, etc.

- <u>Customs</u>: Ramadan, Eid al-Adha, Eid al-Fitr, exclusion of pork in the diet, hijab, etc.

White America:

- <u>Language</u>: English
- <u>Education</u>: European (Greece, Rome) and American history and personalities (Socrates, Einstein, Columbus, Washington, Lincoln, Freud, etc.), French and Spanish languages
- <u>Religion</u>: Christianity
- <u>Common Names</u>: Johnson, Smith, Miller, Dawson, Nicholson, Bateman, Wilson, Jackson, etc.
- <u>Customs</u>: Thanksgiving, Christmas, Easter, 4th of July, Halloween, baseball, etc.

These are some of the most powerful and prominent races and groups of people in the world and culturally, they're all unique, autonomous and independent of each other with the exception of the European connection between America and Russia. In other words, they each embrace their own elements of culture. This doesn't mean that they can't learn, respect or appreciate the cultures of other people but they place their focus and emphasis on their own. As the old saying goes "self-preservation is man's first law".

Culture is the "glue", if you will, that not only holds and binds communities and people together but does so from a generational standpoint creating social and communal continuity, out of which traditions are born. Equally, culture offers individuals a sense of belonging as a member of a particular race/group of people. This is how they learn to respect themselves and each other and develop a collective sense of self-esteem, and more importantly, it is how they build positive relationships among themselves as members of a collective unit.

And any race or ethnic groups of people who embrace their own elements of culture develop a unique bond between themselves as a result of their shared beliefs, experiences, practices and commonalities. No one outside of their race is privy to these cultural exchanges which are essential for building a nation.

It is critically important that we, as African Americans and people of African descent, understand the necessity of culture as other evolved nations of people. Ironically, we were the first people to create a language and the first writing system in the world known as MDW NTW (Medu Netcher). We boast an amazing history and therefore our education should begin with learning about the University of Sankore, Queen Nzinga, Imhotep, and ancient Kemet where our forefathers laid the foundation of modern civilization.

The first religious practice and biblical text was established in ancient Nubia over a thousand years before Judaism, Christianity and Islam existed, and served as the blueprint for how all religions were developed.

Today, however, as a result of our enslavement, African Americans do not have a culture. The various elements that we embrace are the cultural remnants of other people. In other words, our language, education, religion, names and customs are not African-centered and therefore rendering us as a splintered, fragmented and compromised people. Slavery crippled us in more ways than we can imagine because we were "freed" as the cultural step-children of White America.

As a result, we have a multitude of problems plaguing the black community. Our conditions reveal an undeniable cause for concern and require a more sobering insight into the myriad of issues we find ourselves confronted with.

The current state of Black America:

- highest rate of poverty (nearly three times the amount of white America) and close to half of all black children live below poverty
- highest rate of unemployment
- largest percentage of single parent households
- highest divorce rate of all married couples, in addition, 70% of all married black women have been divorced
- highest rate of incarceration for both men and women, although African

Americans only comprise 13% of the US population

- highest student dropout rate, lowest graduation and college enrollment rates
- highest rate of sexually transmitted diseases to include HIV and Aids
- highest rate as victims of crime, to include black on black violence
- disproportionate cases of diabetes, hypertension, colon and different forms of cancer
- highest percentage of people who are stopped, harassed and killed by law enforcement
- highest infant mortality rate
- highest rate of discrimination in employment, voting, housing and healthcare
- highest rate as victims of hate crimes
- highest rate of the homeless population
- lowest age of life expectancy

We must understand that the external conditions of a people are a reflection of their internal state as human beings. Nevertheless, there has never been a successful race in recorded history who engaged in the cultural elements of another people. The language, education, religion, names and customs of a people create the bond that brings about solidarity and cohesiveness within a race.

Consider this, over the last 150 years we have prayed, marched, protested, passed civil rights laws, integrated, created Affirmative Action and voted at the election polls and yet our dire conditions remain the same. We have tried everything except changing ourselves. We can change ourselves by instituting an African-centered cultural orientation and begin a process of renewing who we are.

The T'Challa In You (Positive Self-Images)

As a graduate student at Harvard University, Caroline Wilmuth studied implicit bias and frequently used a well-known riddle in her research: A father and son are in a bad car accident. The father dies at the scene. The son is rushed to the emergency room. The surgeon walks in, sees the boy and says, "I can't operate on that boy-he's my son!" How could this be the case?

The majority of people failed to solve this riddle. The obvious answer is that the surgeon is the boy's mother. For most people this is usually not the first thought that comes to mind. Is he the stepfather or perhaps an uncle who raised him, or the godfather? This is because all people are affected by implicit bias to some degree in America.

Implicit bias, by definition, is assumptions and conclusions we make with our subconscious mind that has been influenced by a plethora of images presented to us throughout our lives. These images help to shape and mold the perceptions we have of ourselves and others.

Implicit bias is what accounts for stereotypes and different forms of prejudices that linger deep within the subconscious mind. The images we are constantly bombarded with, as many as 5,000 a day, are plastered throughout society from television, internet and movies to magazines, schools and religious institutions.

Although each image we see is an "isolated" experience it is the accumulative effect that conditions us to draw certain conclusions on the basis of race, gender, age, height, weight, etc.

As an example, Tamika Cross, a young black doctor on a flight home from Detroit, heard a woman screaming for help for her husband. She immediately took off her headphones, put her tray table up and unbuckled her seatbelt. As a flight attendant called out for medical assistance for the man, who was unresponsive, Cross, a fourth-year resident at McGovern School at the University of Texas Health Science Center, responded by raising her hand.

The flight attended said "oh no sweetie put your hand down, we are looking for actual physicians or nurses or some type of medical personnel, we don't have time to talk to you." Repeated efforts by Dr. Cross to inform the attendant of her medical status were ignored and met with condescending remarks. As a result of Dr. Cross's persistence, she was then asked if she was an "actual physician" followed with the request to see her medical credentials. When a white man approached and identified himself as a doctor, she was then told they no longer needed her help.

Implicit bias is inescapable. It affects everybody-doctors, lawyers, judges, police officers, teachers, etc. whose decisions and opinions can potentially have lasting impressions on our lives and impact us in profound ways. According to the Implicit Association Test, the overwhelming majority of white people see themselves in a far more favorable light than they see African Americans and other minorities. In general, we all see positive images of white people everywhere from politicians, doctors, lawyers, and CEO's to powerful business men and women. In other words, we've been given a steady diet of positive white images our entire lives.

They are the superheroes on TV, supermodels in magazines, and historical figures in the classroom. They represent godly images in bibles and religious institutions. In speaking of religious institutions, most of us cannot begin to imagine the grave psychological damage that is done to the minds of African Americans who are shown images of a white Jesus all of their lives and are taught to believe that Jesus is the "Son of God".

First, it is an emphatic statement that God is white, and secondly, it's a devastating blow to the self-esteem and confidence of blacks and non-white people who, subconsciously, are unable to see God within themselves but recognize the racial traits in every Caucasian man, woman and child.

As Dr. Na'im Akbar states in <u>Chains and Images of Psychological Slavery</u> "if you have internalized the view of the deity and the Creator as being in flesh, having a nationality and physical characteristics different from yourself, then you automatically assume that you are inferior in your own characteristics. The sense of inferiority is not in the form of the "natural humility" which we discussed, but you begin to believe that you have less human potential than one who looks like the image."

On the other hand, the majority of the images we see of African Americans are limited to the athlete, entertainer (singer/rapper, actor, comedian, etc.) hustler and criminal. These images, and the negative/non-intellectual perceptions they convey largely account for the stereotypes, and even more damning, the disparity in the treatment of whites and blacks throughout society.

In healthcare, for example, the Institute of Medicine published a report that reveal minorities are less likely to be given appropriate cardiac medications or to undergo bypass surgery, and less likely to receive kidney dialysis or transplants. By contrast, they are more likely to receive certain less-desirable procedures such as lower limb amputations for diabetes and other conditions.

In law enforcement an exercise was given to police officers where they had to make a split second decision as to whether or not to discharge their firearms. They were shown an equal number of images of whites and blacks as civilians and armed criminals and at a rate of almost two to one the black images were fired upon. In conducting a test on racism, white and black applicants applied for jobs with the same credentials and a large number of the black applicants were rejected when their names sounded "black".

In the court system, African Americans were given the death penalty at a higher rate the more they resembled the stereotypical image of a Black criminal. Whether we are talking about the mass murder of black church members in Charleston, South Carolina, the water crisis in the predominantly black area of Flint, Michigan, or the ongoing killing of unarmed black citizens at the hands of law enforcement this is the influence and danger of implicit bias.

Dr. Gail Christopher, vice president for program strategy at the Kellogg Foundation, explained that centuries of a racial hierarchy in America has left its mark on our society, especially pertaining to how people of color are perceived by whites. "Our society assigns value to groups of people," and added "it is a process that is embedded in the consciousness of Americans and impacted by centuries of bias."

To say this is a perilous situation for African Americans is an understatement. Unfortunately, we are equally exposed to the same images that inflate the egos of white America by placing them on an imaginary pedestal while marginalizing and undervaluing the lives of black people. However, it has the opposite effect because the same images that influence us to respect the intellectual prowess and capabilities of whites lead us to doubt and dismiss our own. We see an expectation of their success in any given capacity but we often fail to see ourselves in the same positive light.

From a psychological standpoint, the countless number of negative images we see of ourselves gives way to forms of self-hatred, a collective sense of low self-esteem, and a general lack of respect for each other. This is what cultivates the "crab in a barrel" syndrome.

We see the effects in the high rate of black on black crime and in various forms of self-degradation. We see it in our inability to form and sustain healthy communities with economic sustainability and in our failed relationships and broken families. It is equally evident in our equating dark skin, full lips and natural features with being unattractive.

In 1954, Dr. Kenneth Clark gained national attention during the Supreme Court case of Brown v. Board of Education as a result of the famous "doll test". Dr. Clark presented identical dolls, one black, one white, to African American children and asked them a series of questions such as "which doll is the good doll", "which one is the nice doll", "which doll is the bad doll", etc. and the vast majority of the black children's responses favored the white doll. In 2005, filmmaker Kiri Davis recreated the doll test for the movie "A Girl Like Me" and 15 out of the 21 African American children chose the white doll over the black doll.

What does all of this mean? It means we must be aware and careful of the images we allow ourselves and our children to be exposed to. We must also be diligent in projecting ourselves with dignity, class and self-respect. It means that we are going to have to turn off the television from time to time and pick up a book with a positive meaning and message. It means that we're going to have to turn the radio from the "feel good" music and listen to black talk radio to find out what's going on in our community.

We have to equally reject images in TV and film that portray blacks as the "funny, loud mouth sidekick", "the gun-toting grandma", "gangster" and negative roles that undermine and undervalue our dignity and intellectual capacity. This is not to say that we don't recognize the brilliance behind some of these performances but we must have an appropriate balance to maintain a healthy sense of who we are.

We must overcome the negative impact of implicit bias that represents a limited, narrow and inaccurate view of who we are as a people. We must celebrate and flaunt our genius, showcase our diversity and highlight our greatness. By doing so, we will defeat the image that perpetuates fear, distrust and inadequacy giving way to low expectations and marginalized efforts. It means that we must choose to embrace the images that are going to reflect the best of who we are and what we're capable of accomplishing.

<u>"We are not Children of a lesser God"</u>- PLO Lumumba

"Seven" (Ka-Maat) is an African American/African diaspora spiritual practice. The basis of the practice was created for several reasons and it is principally the result of an independent study and research of various world religions I conducted beginning with Christianity, Islam, Judaism, Buddhism, Shinto, Hinduism, Yoruba (Orisa Worship) and Egyptian. Further studies would include Mormonism, Jehovah's Witness faith, and the ancient Egyptian text of "The Book of the Dead (The Book of Going Forth by Day)" and "Egyptian Religion" by E.A. Wallis Budge along with a variety of other scholarly works.

During my research of religion, I discovered some things that were encouraging as well as disturbing. What I found encouraging are the many stories of human sacrifice, good conquering evil and colloquiums of righteous judgement. However, what I found disturbing are the roles religions played in the enslavement of African people. Dr. John Henrik Clarke, in *Critical Lessons In Slavery and the Slavetrade*, detail how religions were used to justify slavery at different periods throughout history.

In 1452, for example, Pope Nicolas V issued a papal bull Dum Diversas to sanction the transatlantic slave trade under the authority of the Roman Catholic Church. Consequently, the Europeans termed the slave dungeon built in Mombasa, Kenya as "Fort Jesus" and gave slave ships Christian names such as "the Good Ship Jesus" in hopes that God would bless the journey. They used biblical scriptures to refer to black people as the "cursed seeds of Ham" and other passages that support slavery such Leviticus 25: 44-46:

> "Both thy bondmen, and thy bondmaids, which thou shalt have, shall be of the heathen that are round about you; of them shall ye buy bondmen and bondmaids.
>
> Moreover of the children of the strangers that do sojourn among you, of them shall ye buy, and of their families that are with you, which they begat in your land: and they shall be your possession.
>
> And ye shall take them as an inheritance for your children after you, to inherit them for a possession; they shall be your bondmen forever: but over your brethren the children of Israel, ye shall not rule over another with rigour."

Luke 12: 47-48:

> "And that servant, which knew his lord's will, and prepared not himself, neither did according to his will, shall be beaten with many stripes. But he that knew not and did commit things worthy of stripes, shall be beaten with few stripes."

Thus, religion, through scriptures and leadership, supported the cruel and unjust system that forced our ancestors to suffer and endure the most inhumane and violent experience in recorded history. Additionally, slavery, along with colonialism, left the entire African continent under foreign rule and domination, separated families and utterly destroyed the lives of tens of millions of people. Slavery stripped our ancestors of their language, education, religion, names and customs which are the cultural elements necessary to unify and strengthen a people.

As Dr. Molefi Kete Asante states in his book *Afrocentricy* "All religions rise out of the deification of someone's nationalism. Understand this and you will discern the key to our own victory". In other words, a people's belief in their own God is not only a source of inspiration and empowerment but it's a faith that is defined by their culture.

In Hinduism, for example, the books of the Vedas, the sacred Hindu scriptures, are written in the Hindi language which means according to the Hindu faith it is the language God chose to give his divine message to mankind. Varanasi, a city in north east India, is considered the holy land, and Krishna, the Virgin born savior and deity, is of Indian descent. Undoubtedly, this is the people of India's concept of God, and the cultural undertones we find in Hinduism we find in all faiths.

In Islam, the Prophet Muhammad is considered the last and most important prophet of God (Allah). God spoke to Muhammad in the Arabic language when he received the scriptures of the Holy Quran in his dreams/visions. A holy name in Islam is a traditional Arab name, and according to the faith, the holy cities are Mecca and Medina, a region of Saudi Arabia where Muslims turn to pray and travel to make Hajj. Therefore, it would not be a stretch to say that Islam is an Arab-centered faith.

In Christianity, God spoke the Holy word in the Hebrew language. According to the bible, Jews are God's "Chosen People". The bible references the "God of Abraham, Isaac and Jacob" who were Jews, and Jerusalem, the capital of Israel, is considered the holy city. Jesus, the "Son of God" and "King of Jews" according to the faith, has been depicted in the image of a European Jew since the turn of the 15th century and in the New Testament, Jesus instructs his disciples to only go after the "lost sheep of Israel". Based on the cultural framework it could be surmised that Christianity is a Jewish-centered faith.

It is time for us to embrace an African-centered belief system in order to view God from our own cultural lens as other races of people have done. For us, then, there is no land more holy than the grounds of our ancestors, whether Nubia, Mount Kilimanjaro, the Gold Coast or Jamestown. God, as a concept of either Ra or Olodumare, speaks the holy word in the Yoruba and Kiswahili languages. The rhythmic sound of the drum is sacred and transcendent and we proclaim that all people of African descent are "God's First People" who were chosen to create the human race as we know it, and so it is said.

In other words, we are no less or inferior to any people and having a belief in ourselves is the first step towards our unconditional liberation and commitment in struggle. Free people do not subject themselves to the God and religion of their oppressor. Therefore, faith is not just a mere form of expression or a weekly service of sermons, singing and donations but it's a liberating force of a people's power, identity, and self-affirmation.

It is within this vein that our faith must be born out of the African and African American experience. It is our truth, our story and a celebration of our cultural ethos and ideals as we define our own relationship with God and the means by which it is expressed and honored, in the voice, vision, spirit and interest of our people.

<u>The Significance of Ancient Egypt</u>

There is a consistent reference to ancient Egypt throughout the works of Ka-Maat. From the name of the practice itself to the numerous examples in fundamentals of education, ancient Egypt serves a backdrop to the practice. We reference Egypt, the ancient land originally known as Kemet, for a number of reasons. First, Egypt is in Africa and not somewhere in the Middle East as some would have us to believe.

Secondly, the people inhabiting Egypt today are not the same people who inhabited Egypt 3,000 years ago just as the people we call Americans today are not the same people who were here in the United States 3,000 years ago. Lastly, Egypt is considered the birthplace of civilization.

In the beginning the land was never referred to as Egypt. The word Egypt is of Greek origin from the seventh Century B.C., deriving from the description of the Temple of Ptah at Memphis. Regarded as one of the grandest structures in the Nile Valley, the Greeks referred to this ancient land as Hekaptah. In the Greek language Hekaptah became Aiguptos and under Roman rule the name was Latinized into Aegyptus which became Egypt.

In terms of literature, Egyptians recorded the earliest known writings concerning spirituality and ethics. The concepts of Maat, humans in the image of God, Human Dignity, Judgment after death, Immortality of the soul, Human equality and Social justice all originated in Egypt.

As far as Egypt's African origins, examine the parallels of ancient Egypt to that of Nubia which stretched across from Northern Sudan to Southern Egypt. Nubia was the source of Kemet's early language, philosophy and religion. In many of the hieroglyphic pictorials there are images of African kings, queens and warriors and statues with typical features of dark skin, broad noses, full lips and tightly curled hair. There are also depictions of animals that are indigenous to the African continent; the aardvark, the beisa oryx, and the ostrich.

In the X-ray profile of the mummy of Pharaoh Thutmose IV of the 18th Dynastic Period, the facial image reveals prognathism; a unique facial feature of African people and royalty was primarily established through familial linage. Similarly, if you view the side profile of the Sphinx, the oldest sculpture in Egypt, and draw an imaginary line from the furthest point of its forehead straight down the face you'll notice the mouth protrudes beyond the line because the lower jaw is "jutted". That's how you know the face of the sphinx is the image of an African.

Additionally, Drs. Cheikh Anta Diop and Theophile Obenga laid this issue to rest at the UNESCO

Symposium in 1974, a conference of the world's leading Egyptologists assembled to discuss the race of the Egyptians, by presenting 11 categories of evidence, to include a melanin dosage test that proved the Egyptians were indeed indigenous Africans. More importantly is what the Egyptians said of themselves "we came from the beginning of the Nile where the God Hapi dwells, at the foothills of the mountain of the moon", which is either Kilimanjaro between Kenya and Tanzania or Rwenzori in Uganda.

Egypt, unfortunately, was invaded numerous times beginning with the Hyksos in the 13th dynastic period and later invasions by Persians, Greeks, Romans and Arabs but was originally built and inhabited by an African people.

Henry H. Gorringe, lieutenant commander of the United States Navy made the following statement in 1882:

> Egypt itself is a book of history, one of God's great monumental records....It was the birthplace of literature, the cradle of science and art, the garden and garner of the world....In the branches of decorative art and the science of architecture they were undoubtedly far in advance of us at the present day....The architectural types of all other structures of antiquity sink into insignificance when compared to those of Egypt. The Egyptians

were the first to observe the course of the planets, and their observations led them to regulate the year from the course of the sun. They were a wonderful race, combining within themselves all the branches which adorn, beautify, and add to the reputation of a people when directed in the right channel.

In 1994, the New York Times reported a story by science writer John Noble Wilford concerning a recent discovery near the Nile. It states that the demands for building stones for pyramids and temples led to the opening of many quarries in the low cliffs near the Nile. To make it easier to transport these heavy stones from one of the quarries, the Egyptians built what is probably the world's first paved road. Geologists have found a seven and a half mile stretch of road covered with slabs of sandstone and limestone and logs of petrified wood.

The great statue of the Sphinx is the largest and oldest monument ever sculpted from a single rock. It has the head of a human and the body of reclined lion; it is 240 feet long and 66 feet high. Hundreds of majestically standing Pyramids and Obelisks are not only found in Egypt but in Sudan and Ethiopia.

Monotheism, the belief in one God, was first established in Egypt by Akhenaton just as the 42 Laws of Maat were the earliest recorded writings of moral and ethical guidelines. Kemet has the earliest medical text on record in the form of papyrus and spiritual concepts that predate world religions by more than a thousand years.

What the Egyptians were able to establish in terms of spiritual concepts became the groundwork for developing religions that followed many years later. For instance, the story of Ausar, Aset and Heru is the first story in recorded history of man of a holy royal family, Immaculate Conception, virgin birth, crucifixion and resurrection. Evidence of this Trinity is known to have existed in ancient Nubia as late as 3300 B.C.E. They are described in detail in carvings on the walls of the Temple of Luxor.

The Egyptian influence on religious development is noted in the following examples:

Akhenaton's Hymn (ca.1353 B.C.E.)

The world is in darkness like the dead. Every lion cometh forth from its den: all serpents sting. Darkness reigns. When Thou risest in the horizon...the darkness is banished...Then in all the world they do their work. All trees and plants flourish...the birds flutter in their marshes...All sheep dance upon their feet. The ships sail up stream and down stream alike...The fish in the river leap up before thee: and thy rays are in the midst of the great sea. How manifold are all Thy works!...Thou didst

create the earth according to Thy desire, men
all cattle...all that upon the earth.

RA's Description of His Creation

Thus said Ra, the Lord of All. Lord of the
Utmost Limits, after He had come into being: I
am the one who came into being as Kheper. He
who comes into being and brings into being.
When I came into being being itself came into
being. All beings came into being after I came
into being. Many were the beings that came
forth from the commands of my mouth.
Heaven had not yet come into being. Nor had
earth come into being. Nor had the ground
been created or the things which creep and
crawl upon it. I raised up beings in the
primordial waters as inert things. I found no
place on which to stand. I formed it from the
desire in my heart: I laid the foundation
through Maat. I created forms of every kind.
Many were the forms which issued forth from
the commands of my mouth. Not yet had I
established Shu, the power and principle of light
and air. Nor sent forth Tefnut, the power and
principle of moisture. There existed no one
who acted together with me. I conceived it in
my own heart. And there came into being a
vast number of forms of divine beings as forms

of offspring and forms of their offspring from them...

Hymn to RA (1350 B.C.) From the Papyrus of Hunefer

"Homage to thee, O thou who art Ra when thou risest and Temu when thou settest. Thou risest, thou risest, thou shinest, thou shinest, O thou who art crowned king of the gods. Thou art the Lord of heaven, thou art the Lord of earth; thou art the creator of those who dwell in the heights, and of those who dwell in the depths. Thou art the One God who came into being in the beginning of time. Thou didst create the earth, thou didst fashion man, thou didst make the watery abyss of the sky, thou didst form Hapi, thou didst create the great deep, and thou dost give life unto all that therein is. Thou has knit together the mountains, thou hast made mankind and the beasts of the field to come into being, thou hast made the heavens and the earth. Worshipped be thou whom the goddess Maat embraceth at morn and at eve. Thou dost travel across the sky with thy heart swelling with joy; the great deep of heaven is content there at. The serpent-fiend Nak hath fallen, and his arms are cut off. The Sektet boat receiveth fair winds, and the heart of him that is in the shrine thereof rejoiceth"...

The Book of Prayers and Sacred Praises

Blessed is one who sits in the hands of Amen Ra, for it is He who directs the timid, who rescues the humble and the needy, who gives the breath of life to the one He loves and grants him or her a long life in the West of Thebes.

Oh my God, Lord of Lords, Amen Ra, Lord of Karnak. Give me your hand and save me. Shine upon me and sustain me. You are the only God and there is none like you. You are Ra who rises in the heavens, the God who created men and women.

It is you who hears the prayers of one who calls on Him, who saves a man and woman from the hands of the violent and who makes the Nile rise and flow for those who are in Him. Ra is the perfect guide for everyone.

When he rises men and women live and their hearts are lifted up when they see the one who gives the breath of life to those who are in the egg, who make people and birds to live, who supplies even food for mice in their holes as well as for worms and fleas. May he grant us an honorable burial after an old age, so that we may be safe in His hands.

The Book of Ani

I. Do not go in and out of the court of justice so that your name may not be soiled. Do not contend in a quarrel. Keep silent and it will serve you well. Go not in the presence of a drunkard even if it promises to bring you honor.

II. Pour libation for your father and mother who rest in the valley of the dead. God will witness your action and accept it. Do not forget to do this even when you are away from home. For as you do for your parents, your children will do for you also.

The Book of Ankhsheshonqi

I. Serve God that He may protect you. Serve your brothers and sisters that you may enjoy a good reputation. Serve a wise person that he or she may serve you. Serve one who serves you. Serve any person so you may benefit from it. And serve your mother and father that you may go forward and prosper.

Examine every matter that you may understand it. Do not say I am learned but rather set yourself to become wise. Be gentle and patient, then your character will be beautiful. It is in the development of character that instruction succeeds. Learn the structure and functioning of the sky. Learn the structure and functioning of the earth.

The good fortune of a town is a leader who acts righteously. The good fortune of a temple is its priest. The good fortune of a field is the time it is worked. The good fortune of a storehouse is the stocking of it. And the good fortune of the wise is their excellent advice.

These are merely samples of volumes of scripts that were interpreted by some of the leading authorities in Egyptology, antiquity and linguistics. However, the ancient Egyptian reference throughout the works of Ka-Maat is not done at the exclusion of other African societies and nations and this is certainly not the intent as demonstrated in the section "Basics of Education". Many other countries and regions of African people are included because historical and modern day achievements are truly global from Botswana and Brazil to Jamaica and Harlem, however the development of ancient Egypt is without question significant as the mother of civilization.

"The relationship of a people to their history is the same as the relationship of a child to its mother." – Dr. John Henrik Clarke

Food for Thought

African Americans, as well as most people in America have been taught since early childhood to associate food with fun. Society reinforces this teaching because whenever someone celebrates a birthday they're expected to have cake and ice cream. When you go to the movies it is tradition to have popcorn and soda. When you watch the big game you need chicken wings and pizza and if you go to a cookout it is customary to eat hot dogs and hamburgers. When you need a quick snack the candy bar is the most popular choice. Of course I'm generalizing but the sentiment rings true for many people.

By the time the average person reaches the age of 40 they will have 10 to 15 pounds of undigested red meat in their system because the human body is not designed to properly digest red meat. The idea of casually choosing what, when, where and how to eat has resulted in poor eating habits for many of us over the years.   In the black community we have a health crisis with the number of reported cases of diabetes, hypertension, colon cancer and obesity.

The amount of sodium content in pork, processed meats, fast foods and restaurants are alarming and critical. Many of our young people are having heart attacks and strokes and some of our teenagers and pre-teens are being prescribed medication to treat diabetes and other related health issues before they reach puberty.

How do we combat the growing problem of food related illnesses? We must first understand that the food industry is a multi-billion dollar business. The goal of any business is to amass wealth, and in some cases, even when it comes at the expense of people's health.

Much of the industry's success is by design from a series of food tests, marketing strategies and the use of certain ingredients specifically designed to enhance the flavor and taste of foods. This is why the foods you cook at home can never quite taste like the food prepared in restaurants. The book "Salt Sugar Fat" by Michael Moss details the chemical addiction of food and the scientific approach by the food industry to create products in labs as if food were a new form of heroin or cocaine.

In terms of marketing strategies, several psychological tests have been conducted over the years that show the color red triggers hunger in people. Other tests have shown that people associate the color yellow with sunshine and happiness. For this very reason, you will see the colors red and yellow on the signs of many fast food restaurants across the country from McDonalds and Wendy's to Burger King and Sonic. The colors are also prominent at Denny's and the popular southern fast food chain Hardee's and their affiliate chain as well.

You can also see the color red on the signs of many dine-in restaurants. Also, in many dine-in facilities you will find the color red in prominent places whether it's the carpet on the floor, the paint on the wall, seating booths and tables or all of the above. In fact, many restaurants include the word red in their names from Red Lobster, Red Robin, Red Hot and Blue, to Ruby Tuesdays (ruby is a shade of red). This is not a coincidence but a grand design and over the years it has proven to be enormously successful and it's one of the reasons McDonalds can advertise "Over a Billion Served".

Similar strategies are done with the layout of grocery stores. For example, the main items that most people purchase are meat, eggs, milk, and bread. Therefore, the layout of many grocery stores are designed to place these items at the opposite ends of the store forcing customers to walk past aisles to view other items on sale.

Some stores play soft elevator music to relax customers so they will take their time shopping. Lastly, they place small, inexpensive items at the register like candy bars, breath mints and gum for impulse purchases while waiting in line. And you wonder why you always leave the store with more than what you came to purchase.

In practicing Ka-Maat, we must understand that the purpose of food is to nourish and sustain the body. Food is also our first form of medicine. Food is a medicine because the value of minerals and nutrients from calcium, fiber, protein and potassium that are found in natural fruits and vegetables strengthens the body and helps prevent illness and disease.

Before indulging in food we should ask the questions; what am I eating, why am I eating it, how much of it should I consume, and how will it affect my body? Ultimately, food has the ability to either build or destroy our health. It is up to us to make the right decisions.

The benefits of vegetables

- Broccoli: rich in vitamin A lowers the risk of cancer, primarily cancers of the colon, esophagus, larynx, lung, prostate, oral cavity, pharynx, and stomach. Steam lightly to keep nutrients intact.
- Brussels sprouts: contain vitamins A, C, riboflavin, iron, potassium and fiber; aids the pancreas.
- Cabbage: Kills bacteria and viruses, helps prevent cancer and heal ulcers and stimulates the immune system.

- Cauliflower: rich in vitamin C, potassium and fiber and better for diabetic people than cabbage.
- Kale: leafy green vegetable and rich in calcium, niacin, magnesium, iron and phosphorus.
- Turnip: reduces mucus, helps asthma and bronchitis and relieving sore throats, has high amounts of antioxidants as well as calcium, iron and niacin.
- Watercress: recommended food for anemia, calcium deficiencies, thyroid, liver and pancreas problems and arthritis.
- Green Beans: rich in vitamins A, B-complex and C, chlorophyll, carbohydrates, calcium, phosphorus, copper and cobalt.
- Carrots: powerful anti-oxidant builds healthy skin, improves eyesight and is heart healthy.
- Chili Peppers: helps dissolve blood clots and contains capsaicin which works as a pain killer.
- Collards: improves nervous system, respiratory system, urinary system, helps osteoporosis, arthritis and cancer.
- Corn: a brain food that helps build bone and muscle, rich in vitamins A,B, and C, potassium, iron, zinc, magnesium and fiber.
- Onions: a food of the garlic family aids in Hay Fever, asthma, Bronchitis, High Blood Pressure and is a potent anti-oxidant.
- Peas: helps prevent ulcers, lowers blood pressure as well as blood cholesterol and

contains no fat (buy fresh peas only, no
canned).

- Potatoes: rich in vitamins, minerals, proteins, and are high in potassium. A cancer fighting food, potatoes help to balance alkalinity and acidity in the body.
- Tomatoes: aid in the cleansing of toxins and lowers the risk of cancer but should be avoided by people who suffer from arthritis.
- Yams: sweet potatoes help stave off lung cancer, even for ex-smokers. The darker orange coloring indicates a higher concentration of disease fighting carotenoids.
- Garlic: a wonder food known for preventive and healing properties. Garlic lowers the LDL, helps with arthritis and the immune system, recommended for everyday consumption and comes in odorless form as well.

The benefits of fruits

- Apples: contain 84% pure water, high in protein, minerals, carbohydrates, iron, potassium and vitamins A, B and C.
- Apricots: excellent source of fiber, high in carotene and its seeds are used in some cancer treatments.
- Bananas: low in fat, rich in potassium and vitamin C, helps with High Blood Pressure, heart

disorders, nerves, ulcers and a variety of other ailments.

- Blueberries: high in manganese and vitamin A, highly recommended fruit in the prevention of cancer and other diseases.
- Cherries: excellent for gout and arthritis, removes toxic waste from tissues and aids the gall bladder and liver function.
- Cranberry: as a juice, cranberries help control bladder infections and are high in vitamin C.
- Grapes: helps combat toxins, increase energy and cleanses tissues and glands.
- Grapefruit: the whole fruit, pectin, pulp and fibrous content are important. High in potassium and vitamin C with no fat, its' seeds aid in healing candida and other infections.
- Lemons and Pineapple: lemons are a liver stimulant and a solvent for uric acid and other toxins. Fresh pineapples contain manganese which is essential in metabolizing protein and carbohydrates.
- Cantaloupe: rich in vitamins A and C, potassium and low in calories per serving.
- Oranges: contains high amounts of vitamins C and A.
- Pomegranate: the seeds are used to aid against certain forms of cancers.
- Strawberries: contain high amounts of vitamin C and fiber. High in potassium and a good anti-oxidant. Protects against viruses and cancer.

- Watermelon: a natural diuretic, watermelon purifies blood and cleanses tissues and is rich in vitamin C.

<u>Alternative Soul Food Recipes</u>

I N G R E D I E N T S
<u>CATFISH STEW</u>
<u>*with* RICE</u>

2 medium potatoes
1, 14½-ounce can
tomatoes, cut up
1 cup chopped onion
1, 8-ounce bottle (1
cup) clam juice or water
1 cup water
2 cloves garlic, minced
½ head cabbage,
coarsely chopped
1 lb. catfish fillets
1½ tablespoon
Hot 'n Spicy Seasoning
(see recipe on page 19)
sliced green onion for
garnish (optional)
2 cups hot, cooked rice
(white or brown)
1 Peel potatoes and cut into quarters. In a large pot,
combine potatoes, tomatoes and their juice, onion,
clam juice, water, and garlic. Bring to boiling;
reduce heat. Cook, covered, over medium-low heat
for 10 minutes.
2 Add cabbage. Return to boiling. Reduce heat; cook,

covered, over medium-low heat for 5 minutes, stirring occasionally.

3 Meanwhile, cut fillets into 2-inch lengths. Coat with Hot 'n Spicy Seasoning. Add fish to vegetables. Reduce heat; simmer, covered, for 5 minutes or until fish flakes easily with a fork.

4 Serve in soup plates, garnished with sliced green onion. Top with an ice cream scoop of hot, cooked rice. Or, ladle stew over hot, cooked rice in soup plates and garnish with green onion

BAKED Fried
Chicken Breast
with MIXED VEGETABLES

1 Pre-heat oven to 350°. Spray a medium baking pan with cooking spray. On waxed paper, mix bread crumbs, cheese, cornmeal, and ground red pepper.

2 In pie plate, beat egg white and salt. Dip each piece of chicken in egg white mixture, then coat with bread crumb mixture. Place chicken in pan; spray lightly with cooking spray.

3 Bake chicken for 30 minutes or until coating is crisp and juices run clear when chicken is pierced with the tip of a knife. Add mixed vegetables to chicken. Bake for 5 more minutes. Serve with garlic mashed potatoes (page 28).

non-stick cooking spray

½ cup plain dried bread
crumbs

½ cup grated Parmesan
cheese

2 tablespoons cornmeal

½ teaspoon ground red

pepper
1 large egg white
½ teaspoon salt
1½ lbs. boneless,
skinless chicken breast
3 cups mixed
vegetables

20 MINUTE
CHICKEN CREOLE

1 Spray deep skillet with non-stick spray coating.
Preheat pan over high heat. Cook chicken in hot
skillet, stirring for 3 to 5 minutes or until no longer
pink.
2 Reduce heat. Add tomatoes and their juice,
low-sodium chili sauce, green pepper, celery, onion,
garlic, basil, parsley, crushed red pepper, and salt.
Bring to boiling; reduce heat and simmer covered
for 10 minutes. Serve over hot, cooked rice or
whole wheat pasta.
4 medium chickens
breast halves
(1½ lbs. total) skinned,
boned, and cut into
1-inch strips
1, 14-ounce can
tomatoes,
cut up
1 cup low-sodium
chili sauce
1½ cups chopped green
pepper (1 large)
½ cup chopped celery

¼ cup chopped onion
2 cloves garlic, minced
1 tablespoon chopped
fresh basil or 1 teaspoon
dried basil, crushed
1 tablespoon chopped
fresh parsley or
1 teaspoon dried parsley
¼ teaspoon crushed red
pepper
¼ teaspoon salt
non-stick cooking spray
NUTRITION CONTENT
Per Serving
Makes 4 servings
calories: 255
total fat: 3g
saturated fat: 0.8g
carbohydrates: 16g
protein: 31g
cholesterol: 100mg
sodium: 465mg
dietary fiber: 1.5g
To reduce sodium, try low-sodium
canned tomatoes.

SPAGHETTI
***with* TURKEY MEAT SAUCE**

NUTRITION CONTENT

Per Serving
Makes 6 servings
calories: 330

total fat: 5g
saturated fat: 1.3g
carbohydrates: 42g
protein: 29g
cholesterol: 60mg
sodium: 280mg
dietary fiber: 2.7g

1 lb. ground turkey
1, 28-ounce can
tomatoes, cut up
1 cup finely chopped
green pepper
1 cup finely chopped
onion
2 cloves garlic, minced
1 teaspoon dried
oregano, crushed
1 teaspoon black
pepper
1 lb. spaghetti
non-stick cooking spray

1 Spray a large skillet with non-stick spray coating. Preheat over high heat. Add turkey; cook, stirring occasionally, for 5 minutes. Drain fat.

2 Stir in tomatoes with their juice, green pepper, onion, garlic, oregano, and black pepper. Bring to boiling; reduce heat. Simmer, covered, for 15 minutes, stirring occasionally.

3 Remove cover; simmer for 15 minutes more. (For a creamier sauce, give sauce a whirl in a blender or food processor.)

4 Meanwhile, cook spaghetti according to package directions; drain well. Serve sauce over spaghetti with crusty, whole-grain bread.

SUCCOTASH

1 Combine lima beans, margarine, corn, tomatoes, onions, Tabasco sauce, salt, and pepper in a pan.
2 Bring to a boil, reduce heat, and simmer for 20 minutes.
3 Add okra and cook for 10 more minutes.
10-ounce baby lima
beans (frozen)
2 tablespoons
margarine (such as
Promise™ 60% spread)
10-ounce whole kernel
corn (frozen)
10-ounce cut okra
15-ounce canned
tomatoes (undrained)
½ cup chopped onions
Tabasco sauce to taste
Salt and black pepper
to taste

NEW ORLEANS
RED BEANS

1 Pick through beans to remove bad beans; rinse thoroughly. In a 5-quart pot, combine beans, water, onion, celery, and bay leaves. Bring to boiling; reduce heat. Cover and cook over low heat for about 1½ hours or until beans are tender. Stir and mash some of the beans against side of the pan to thicken the mixture.
2 Add green pepper, garlic, parsley, thyme, salt, and

black pepper. Cook, uncovered, over low heat until creamy, about 30 minutes. Remove bay leaves.
3 Serve over hot, cooked brown rice, if desired.
1 lb. dry red beans
2 quarts water
1½ cups chopped onion
1 cup chopped celery
4 bay leaves
1 cup chopped sweet
green pepper
3 tablespoons
chopped garlic
3 tablespoons
chopped parsley
2 teaspoons dried
thyme, crushed
1 teaspoon salt
1 teaspoon
Black pepper

MIXED GREENS

1 Rinse greens well, removing stems. In a large pot of boiling water, cook greens rapidly, covered, over medium heat for about 25 minutes or until tender.
2 Serve with some of the pot liquor (liquid from the cooked greens). If desired, cut greens in pan with a sharp knife and kitchen fork before serving.
2 bunches mustard
greens or kale
2 bunches turnip greens
pepper to taste
(optional)
1 teaspoon salt,

or to taste (optional)

Beet greens like collards, mustard and turnip greens are a good source of potassium which helps maintain healthy blood pressure. Potassium counteracts the effect of sodium on blood pressure. Too much sodium causes the blood pressure to rise. Dark green leafy vegetables are naturally high in potassium and low in sodium.

GARLIC MASHED POTATOES

1 Peel potatoes; cut in quarters. Cook, covered, in a small amount of boiling water for 20 to 25 minutes or until tender. Remove from heat. Drain. Cover the pot.
2 Meanwhile, in a saucepan over low heat, cook garlic in milk until garlic is soft, about 30 minutes.
3 Add milk-garlic mixture and white pepper to potatoes. Beat with an electric mixer on low speed or mash with a potato masher until smooth.
Use low-fat (1% or 2%) or nonfat/skim milk instead of whole milk.
1 lb. potatoes (2 large)
2 cups skim milk
2 large cloves garlic, chopped
½ teaspoon white pepper

HONEY CANDIED YAMS

1 Wash and peel yams. Cut in quarters and then cut into 2 pieces each. Rinse pieces.

2 Place yams, honey, water, nutmeg, margarine, and flavor in a sauce pan and heat until boiling.
3 Turn heat down to medium, cover and let simmer until all water boils out and the sauce is syrupy.

3 small yams
¼ cup honey
½ cup water
¼ teaspoon ground
nutmeg
1 tablespoon
light margarine
¼ teaspoon lemon flavor

PASTA SALAD

1 Cook pasta according to package directions. Drain; cool.
2 In a large bowl stir together yogurt, mustard, and herb seasoning. Add pasta, celery, and green onion; mix well. Chill at least 2 hours.
3 Just before serving, carefully stir in shrimp and tomatoes.
8-ounce (2½ cups)
medium shell pasta
1, 8-ounce carton (1
cup) plain nonfat yogurt
2 tablespoons
spicy brown mustard
2 tablespoons salt-free
herb seasoning
1½ cups chopped
celery
1 cup sliced green
onion

1 lb. cooked small
shrimp
3 cups coarsely
chopped tomatoes
(about 3 large)

GARDEN
POTATO SALAD

1 In a blender, blend cottage cheese, milk, lemon
juice, vinegar, celery seed, dillweed, dry mustard,
and white pepper until smooth. Chill for 1 hour.
2 Scrub potatoes; boil in jackets until tender. Cool;
peel. Cut into ½-inch cubes. Add celery, green
onion, and parsley.
3 Pour chilled cottage cheese mixture over vegetables;
mix well. Chill at least 30 minutes before serving.
3 lbs. potatoes (6 large)
1 cup chopped celery
½ cup sliced green
onion
2 tablespoons
chopped parsley
DRESSING
1 cup low-fat cottage
cheese
¾ cup skim milk
3 tablespoons
lemon juice
2 tablespoons
cider vinegar
½ teaspoon
celery seed
½ teaspoon dill weed

½ teaspoon dry mustard
½ teaspoon
white pepper

DESSERTS

FRUIT SALAD

1 Wash all fresh fruits well. Slice grapes. Slice
strawberries
and remove stems. Peel orange, slice and
remove seeds and membranes, and cut into bite size
pieces. Peel apples, remove core, and cut into
small pieces. Combine fruit in large bowl.
2 Add fruit cocktail.
3 Stir until all fruit is mixed. Level the top and sprinkle
coconut. Chill. Serve.
1 lb. seedless black
grapes
6 medium red apples
1 pint strawberries
6 medium oranges
16-ounce can of fruit
cocktail, packed in juice
1 cup coconut
(shredded)

WINTER *and*
SUMMER CRISP

1 In a medium bowl, combine sugar, flour, and
lemon peel; mix well. Add apples and cranberries;
stir to mix. Spoon into a 6-cup baking dish.
2 In a small bowl, combine oats, brown sugar, flour,
and cinnamon. Add melted margarine; stir to mix.

Sprinkle topping over filling.
3 Bake in a 375° oven for 40 to 50 minutes or until filling is bubbly and top is brown. Serve warm or at room temperature.

FILLING

½ cup granulated sugar
3 tablespoons
all-purpose flour
1 teaspoon
grated lemon peel
5 cups unpeeled, sliced
apples
1 cup cranberries

TOPPING

$^2/^3$ cup rolled oats
$^1/^3$ cup packed brown
sugar
¼ cup whole wheat
flour
2 teaspoons
ground cinnamon
3 tablespoons
soft margarine, melted

SWEET POTATO CUSSTARD

1 In a medium bowl, stir together sweet potato and banana. Add milk, blending well. Add brown sugar, egg yolks, and salt, mixing thoroughly.
2 Spray a 1-quart casserole with non-stick spray coating. Transfer sweet potato mixture to casserole.
3 Combine raisins, sugar, and cinnamon; sprinkle over top of sweet potato mixture. Bake in a preheated

300° F oven for 45 to 50 minutes or until a
knife inserted near center comes out clean.
1 cup cooked, mashed
sweet potato
½ cup mashed banana
(about 2 small)
1 cup evaporated
skim milk
2 tablespoons
packed brown sugar
2 beaten egg yolks
(or 1$^{1}/^{3}$-cup egg
substitute)
½ teaspoon salt
¼ cup raisins
1 tablespoon sugar
1 teaspoon ground
cinnamon
Non-stick cooking spray

BREAD PUDDING
with APPLE RAISIN SAUCE

1 Preheat the oven to 350° F. Spray an 8-inch x
8-inch baking dish with vegetable oil spray. Lay
the slices of bread in the baking dish in two rows,
overlapping them like shingles.
2 In a medium mixing bowl, beat together the egg,
egg whites, milk, ¼ cup sugar, brown sugar, and
vanilla. Pour the egg mixture over the bread.
3 In a small bowl, stir together the cinnamon,
nutmeg, cloves, and 2 teaspoons sugar. Sprinkle
the spiced sugar over the bread pudding. Bake the
pudding for 30 to 35 minutes, until it has browned

on top and is firm to the touch.
4 Serve warm or at room temperature, with warm
apple-raisin sauce.
APPLE RAISIN SAUCE
Stir all the ingredients together in a medium saucepan.
Bring to a simmer over low heat. Let the sauce simmer
5 minutes. Serve warm.
10 slices whole wheat
bread
1 egg
3 egg whites
1½ cups skim milk
¼ cup granulated sugar
¼ cup brown sugar
1 teaspoon vanilla extract
½ teaspoon cinnamon
¼ teaspoon nutmeg
¼ teaspoon cloves
2 teaspoons sugar

APPLE RAISIN SAUCE

1¼ cups apple juice
½ cup apple butter
2 tablespoons molasses
½ cup raisins
¼ teaspoon ground
cinnamon
¼ teaspoon ground
nutmeg
½ teaspoon
orange peel (optional)

The Importance of Sleep

The International Agency for Research on Cancer and The American Cancer Society recently announced they would most likely add nighttime shift work to their list of "known and probable carcinogens". This cancer-link impacts as many as 15 to 20 million Americans and millions more worldwide. According to a recent report by the Bureau of labor and Statistics, African Americans, at an alarming rate of 20.8%, worked more mid-night and irregular shifts than any other race.

In recent years, several studies have found that women and men working at night for many years substantially increase their risk of breast and prostate cancer, respectively.   Scientists suspect that mid-night shift work is dangerous because it disrupts the circadian rhythm, the body's biological clock. The hormone melatonin, which can suppress tumor development, is normally produced at night. Light shuts down melatonin production so people working in artificial light at night may have a lower melatonin level which is believed to raise their chances of developing cancer.

Sleep deprivation may also be a factor in cancer risk. People who work at night are not usually able to completely reverse their day and night cycles. Not getting enough sleep makes your immune system vulnerable to attack, and less able to fight off potentially cancerous cells. Confusing your body's natural rhythm can also lead to a breakdown of other essential tasks. "Certain processes like cell division and DNA repair happen at regular times" according to Mark Rea, director of the Light Research Center at Rensselaer Polytechnic Institute in New York.

Quality sleep at the right time helps protect your mental and physical health. How you feel when you awake depends in part to how well you slept during the night. During sleep the body works to support healthy brain function and with children it also helps their growth and development. Studies show that sleeping well at night improve our ability to learn and comprehend. Sleep is the body's' renewal process from day to day and 8 hours is recommended for both children and adults.

Sleep helps to heal and repair heart and blood vessels, repair cells and strengthen the immune system. Whereas sleep deficiency can lead to an increased risk of heart disease, kidney disease, blood pressure, diabetes and stroke. Additionally, the lack of sleep increases the risk of obesity, especially in teenagers. Good sleep improves our mood and allows us to be productive and alert throughout the day without the consumption of caffeine and other artificial means and byproducts. Thus, a positive mind-set underscores the essence of spirituality.

The Wonders of Water

Water is the body's principal chemical component and compromises 60 percent of your body weight. Every system in the body depends on water, from flushing toxins out of vital organs to carrying nutrients to cells. An adequate amount of water keeps the body hydrated and replenishes cells to sustain energy throughout the day. It equally aids in digestion, maintaining body temperature, circulation and preventing dry mouth which can cause breath odor.

Water has to be replenished throughout the day because the body loses water in a variety of ways. For example, we lose water through perspiration, urination, breath and bowel movements. According to the Institute of Medicine, men should consume roughly 3 liters (13 cups) of water a day and women should drink 2.2 liters (9 cups) of water daily. By replacing higher calorie options such as soda, ice tea and other sweet beverages, water can also aid in weight loss.

Facts about water;

- Its' quality is determined by the level of pollutants that feed into the water supply.
- The purity and safety of tap water can depend on where you live.
- Bottled water is not a recommended alternative because of unsafe levels of contaminants and excess plastic.

- Filtered water at home is better than bottled water from the store.
- The availability of fresh water in the world is becoming scarce and more critical each year.

Benefits of Exercise

Exercise is an essential part of a healthy lifestyle. Everyone from young children to senior citizens is encouraged to engage in physical activity every day. This can include a simple walk or run, basic calisthenics such as jump rope, pushups and sit-ups or an all-out intense workout in the gym if you're able to do so. Regardless of which workout you choose, unless you're injured or have physical limitations, the only thing unacceptable is doing nothing.

The benefits of exercise are too many to name. However, I will touch on a few essentials such as strengthening the heart and lungs and improving blood circulation. It builds muscle and endurance and helps to aid the immune system. Exercise also helps us lose and maintain weight, get into physical shape, and studies show that consistent working out can improve self-esteem and confidence which is essential to spirituality.

Meditation

Meditation is a time of peace for the mind and soul. It is the opportunity to momentarily remove yourself from the everyday hustle and bustle of life. Additionally, it is a quiet time to reflect, think and plan.

Sakyong Mipham Rinpoche states "In mindfulness, or shamatha, meditation, we are trying to achieve a mind that is stable and calm. What we begin to discover is that this calmness or harmony is a natural aspect of the mind. Through mindfulness practice we are just developing and strengthening it, and eventually we are able to remain peacefully in our mind without struggling. Our mind naturally feels content".

There are certain conditions that are helpful in the practice of meditation. When we create the environment it's easier to practice. It is good if the place where you meditate has a feeling of peace and tranquility or spiritual significance. To this end, you should not meditate in a place that is noisy or distracting or provoke adverse emotions such as stress, anger or frustration. If you are disturbed or irritated, then your meditative state is going to be affected.

Similar to Ka-Maat, the Buddhist approach is that the mind and body are connected. The energy flows better when the body is erect, and if not, the flow is changed and that directly affects your thought process. It is believed that posture actually affects the mind.

Therefore, people who need to use a chair for meditation should sit upright with their feet touching the ground. Anyone using a meditation cushion such as a zafu or gomden should find a comfortable position with legs crossed and hands resting palm-down on your thighs. Keep in mind; the hips are neither rotated forward too much, which creates tension, nor tilted back so you start slouching. You should have a feeling of stability and strength.

When we sit down the first thing we need to do is to really inhabit our body—really have a feeling and begin to notice the breathing. The feeling of breath is very important. The breath should not be forced it should be natural breathing. As the breath is going in and out, you become more relaxed each time you exhale. Every time you breathe, come back to the situation at hand and stay in the present state of mind. Remain focused as you continue breathing in consistent, natural breaths.

Sakyong Mipham Rinpoche further states "Each meditation session is a journey of discovery to understand the basic truth of who we are". He continues, "Mindfulness practice is simple and completely feasible. And because we are working with the mind that experiences life directly, just by sitting and doing nothing, we are doing a tremendous amount".

It is advised that meditation should be done for short periods of time between ten and fifteen minutes, once or twice a day. However, it is important to have a sense of discipline to focus on the mind and nothing else.

Fasting and Prayer

Fasting, which often coincides with meditation, is the abstinence of food for a period of time that varies from predetermined hours to a day or more. Most people may be surprised but the more often you fast the easier it becomes. Ultimately fasting is symbolic of sacrificing for a cause or commitment and requires discipline and a certain amount of intellectual aptitude. We recommend fasting once a week.

Prayer is offering praise and thanks to the Creator, and to seek guidance and direction for yourself and others. It also presents opportunities to self-reflect, to acknowledge our shortcomings and fallibilities and ask for ways to strengthen our weaknesses. During holidays, family gatherings, and special occasions it is befitting to acknowledge and honor the memories of our ancestors and loved ones who have transitioned in prayer, to remember their presence and continuous meaning and significance in our lives.

Prayer should be a manifestation of sincerity, devotion and spiritual consciousness. We conclude our prayers with "asante sana" which means "thank you" in Swahili, the most widely used language on the African continent. We choose not to say "amen" because it originated from the name of the African God Amen Ra and in the hands of non-African people it was reduced to a salutation at the end of a Christian prayer. It is not only disrespectful but demeaning to the belief of

African people which is why asante sana is more appropriate.

We refer to God as either "God", "Creator" or "Mother-Father God". More importantly, we don't use single male or female pronouns for God such as He or Him, She or Her. The intent here is to maintain a holistic concept of the Creator without eliminating 50% of possibilities with gender references. To say God is a male is to say God is not a female and therefore has no feminine qualities or nature, reducing God to an image no different from that of mortal man. It is equally like saying God is "right handed" which would imply that God's "left hand" is weaker and less significant.

Therefore, a full and complete concept is the most powerful image of the Creator that can be conveyed. Thus, the greater the image we have of God the greater belief we have in God's power and ability.

We must understand that truth is not something that we can compromise. Let us do good because good is what is needed in the world. Let us be righteous in all things, and spread positivity everywhere we go. Let us establish peace and harmony in our lives and in our relationships with others. We should always be just in our actions and understand the decision to do right or wrong is a conscious determination. Honor and learn from the elders, be responsible for the children, care for those who are unable to care for themselves, and respect all people.

"Surely, Maat (right-doing) is for eternity. It goes to the grave with one who does it. When he is buried and the earth envelopes him, his name is not erased from the face of the earth. He is remembered because of his goodness. Speak truth and do justice. For Maat (right-doing) is mighty. It is great; it endures; its worth has been proved and it leads one to blessedness. Wrongdoing does not achieve its goal, but one who is upright reaches dry land." – Book of Khun-Anup from *The Husia* by Dr. Maulana Karenga

<u>**Quotes of Inspiration and Wisdom**</u>

- I've learned that people will forget what you said, people will forget what you did, but people will never forget how you made them feel.

- We see no need for the setting apart one day in seven as holy, for to us all days belong to God.   - Ohiyesa, Dakotah Sioux

- No part of our legacy is more valuable than the unique ethical teaching of the Odu Ifa, the sacred text of our Yoruba ancestors, that we and all humans are divinely chosen to bring good into the world and that this is the fundamental meaning and mission of human. – Dr. Maulana Karenga

- Africans in the United States must remember that the slave ships brought no West Indians, no Caribbeans, no Jamaicans or Trinidadians or Barbadians to this hemisphere. The slave ships brought only African people and most of us took the semblance of nationality from the places where slave ships dropped us off. – Dr. John Henrik Clarke

- It is the wise person who sees near and far as the same, does not despise the small or value the great. – Chuang Tzu

- Each soul must meet the morning sun, the new sweet earth, and the Great Silence alone. – Ohiyesa, Dakotah Sioux

- It is never okay to look down on someone unless you're giving them a hand to pull them up.

- Being male and female doesn't make anyone a man or a woman. Being responsible, showing respect for yourself and others, having dignity and humility, and the courage to stand for truth is what makes a man and a woman.

- Peace is not merely the absence of tension it is the presence of justice. – Dr. Martin Luther King Jr.

- Do not be proud and arrogant with your knowledge. Consult and converse with the ignorant and the wise, for the limits of art are not reached. No artist ever possesses that perfection to which he should aspire. Good speech is more hidden than greenstone (emeralds), yet it may be found among maids at the grindstones. – Ptah Hotep

- A wise man is not someone who learns from their own mistakes but from the mistakes of others.

- Self-discipline is a critical aspect of intelligence but there is no intelligence without consciousness.

- History shows that it does not matter who is in power...those who have not learned to do for themselves and have to depend solely on others never obtain any more rights or privileges in the end than they had in the beginning. - Dr. Carter G. Woodson

- If you can walk you can dance. If you can talk you can sing.- Zimbabwe

- The tree-knot spoils the axe; hunger spoils love. – Efik, Nigeria

- Children are the reward of life. – Zaire

- Calm down, little brother, time heals all wounds. No matter how much one is weeping, the moon always follows the sun. Eat your bananas and fresh leaves, and

don't cry anymore, because forever and
ever the moon will follow the sun. - Zaire

- Do not scheme against people. God will
  punish accordingly; if a man says, "I shall
  live by scheming," he will lack bread for his
  mouth. If a man says, "I will be rich;" he will
  have to say, "My cleverness has trapped
  me." If he says, "I will trap for myself" he
  will not be able to say, "I trapped for my
  profit." If a man says, "I will rob someone,"
  he will end by being given to a stranger.
  People's schemes do not prevail. God's
  command is what prevails. Therefore, live
  in the midst of peace. What God gives
  comes by itself. – Ptah Hotep

- If you want to have perfect conduct, to be
  free from every evil, then above all guard
  against the vice of greed. Greed is a
  grievous sickness that has no cure. There is
  no treatment for it. It embroils fathers,
  mothers and the brothers of the mother. It
  parts the wife from the husband. Greed is a
  compound of all the evils. It is a bundle of
  all hateful things. That person endures
  whose rule is rightness, who walks a
  straight line, for that person will leave a
  legacy by such behavior. On the other

hand, the greedy has no tomb. – Ptah
Hotep

- All religions rise out of the deification of
someone's nationalism. Understand this
and you will discern the key to our own
victory. – Dr. Molefi Kete Asante

- Afrocentricity is the belief in the centrality
of Africans in postmodern history. It is our
history, our mythology, our creative motif,
and our ethos exemplifying our collective
will. On the basis of our story, we build
upon the works of our ancestors who gave
signs toward our humanizing function. Nija
teaches in quarter 4, verse 4, "and you are
meant to be a sign for the world". The
songs, poems, stories, sermons, and
proverbs demonstrate our ancestors'
inexorable movement toward the
humanizing function, more fitted by a
higher civilization, a peaceful agrarian
mythology, and spiritual explorations, our
people affirm in the Diaspora and on the
continent the mission of spirit. – Dr. Molefi
Kete Asante

- To commemorate the past is also to
commemorate the struggles and deeds of
the people, to honor the narrative of their

struggle to shape their world in their own image and interest; that is to say, make it mirror their values and serve their basic and higher needs. Here, history as memory- both sacred and secular-is important and compelling. And one is morally compelled to remember the struggle and achievement of the ancestors. For it is they who paved the path for the living and the yet-unborn, who left the model and legacy of tradition; the tradition which grounds the people, provides cultural authority and measures the cultural authenticity of all that is thought or done. To remember, then, is to honor and preserve; to forget is to violate memory, dishonor the dead and deprive the living and the yet unborn of a rich and irreplaceable legacy. - Kwanzaa, Commemoration of the Past-
Dr. Maulana Karenga

- Speak truth in your house that the princes of the earth may respect you. Righteousness is fitting for a ruler. For it is the front of the house that inspires respect in the back. Do that which is right that you may live long upon the earth. Comfort the weeper and oppress not the widow. Drive no one away from the property of his or her father. Defraud not the nobles of their property. Beware of punishing unjustly. Do not kill for it will not profit you…- Book of Kheti as quoted by Dr. Maulana Karenga in the Husia

- Education is the passport to the future, for tomorrow belongs to those who prepare for it today.- Malcolm X

- Be the change you wish to see in the world.- Gandhi

- A man who stands for nothing will fall for anything.- Malcolm X

- Injustice anywhere is a threat to justice everywhere. - Dr. Martin Luther King, Jr.

- The hottest place in Hell is reserved for those who remain neutral in times of great moral conflict. – Dr. Martin Luther King, Jr.

- It is not who you attend school with but who controls the schools you attend.- Nikki Giovani

- Invest in the human soul. Who knows, it might be a diamond in the rough. – Mary McLeod Bethune

- Every great dream begins with a dreamer. Always remember, you have within you the strength, the patience, and the passion to reach for the stars to change the world. – Harriet Tubman

- We have to talk about liberating minds as well as liberating society. – Angela Davis

- There is no future for a people who deny their past. – Adam Clayton Powell, Jr.

- A great history reflects the greatness of a people. It is their reputation chiseled in time to speak of who they are and what they are capable of. Thus enshrining every individual accomplishment with a timeless luster.

- Human beings cannot be willed and molded into non-existence. – Angela Davis

- It is time for parents to teach young people early on that in diversity there is beauty and there is strength. We all should know that diversity makes for a rich tapestry, and we must understand that all the treads of that tapestry are equal in value no matter their color. –
Dr. Maya Angelou

- A man with wisdom is better off than a stupid man with any amount of charm and superstition. – African Proverb

- To rise, we must hold a vision of ourselves spreading our wings, reaching for the sky saying, "I can"…To everything there is an on. This time it's our time to rise. – Susan Taylor

- For Africa to me…is more than a glamorous fact. It is historical truth. No man can know where he is going unless he knows exactly where he has been and exactly how he arrived at his present place. – Dr. Maya Angelou

- From what we get, we can make a living; what we give, however, makes   a life. – Arthur Ashe

- All people have the right and responsibility to look at God through their own imagination and address God in a language of their own creation. - Dr. John Henrik Clarke

- A mind with a body improperly nourished is as deficient as a body with a mind

inadequately conscious is handicapped. –
Dr. Na'im Akbar

- Setbacks in life are nothing more than
  stumbling blocks to climb upon. Once you
  do you'll be that much closer to your goals.

- We can't stand ourselves if we're busy
  holding someone else down.

- If this world had a righteous plan for you
  and me, we would have been taught early
  on how to give love to ourselves in a real
  way … How to delight in our collective
  history…But the world doesn't offer that-
  particularly to Black folk. We must struggle
  and invent to learn it on our own. – Susan
  Taylor

- If you have no confidence in self, you are
  twice defeated in the race of life.- Marcus
  Garvey

- If you are a man who leads, a man who
  controls the affairs of many, then seek the
  most perfect way of performing your
  responsibility so that your conduct will be
  blameless. Great is Maat (truth, justice and
  righteousness). It is everlasting. Maat has
  been unchanged since the time of Asar. To

create obstacles to the following of laws, is
to open a way to a condition of violence.
The transgressor of laws is punished,
although the greedy person overlooks this.
Baseness may obtain riches, yet crime never
lands its wares on the shore. In the end
only Maat lasts. Man says, "Maat is my
father's ground." – Ptah Hotep

- Everyone has a right to their own beliefs
but how do we honor the memory of our
ancestors if we embrace the religion of the
people who enslaved them? – Mudada
Abdu

Charity

Charity is extremely important in our personal and collective maturity and growth. We give out of freewill with the sole intent to help and assist others in need. However, we do not subscribe to charity as a means of self service, to stick out our chests and pat ourselves on the back. In other words, we do not idly sit and ignore the suffering of others until "Thanksgiving" and "Christmas" so we can give in order to feel good about ourselves.

Ironically, many people will only give during the holidays as a form of self-affirmation but homelessness, hunger and despair have no season. We give as we can, whenever we can because it is the right thing to do.

Charity can be in the form of money but can also include volunteering. We can volunteer our time to help in schools, assist students, and help the elderly and disabled. Become involved in Big Brother and Big Sister mentoring programs. We can also coach or provide transportation for recreational sports teams in the community. If we are unable to provide services outside the home there are ways we can work in the home such as online tutoring or form online study groups to read and share positive and valuable information.

Being charitable has a wide-range of meaning and can include blood donation and even signing up to be an organ donor. Volunteering at a hospital, making dinner for a sick person and working in a soup kitchen are all ways you can donate your time and resources. You can assist the elderly by driving them to the grocery store or doctor's office. You can also clean out your closet and donate to nonprofits and shelters that are constantly looking for used books, clothes and other items.

Giving circles, where people pool money as a group and jointly decide where to put it is one way to make a large donation and subsequently a huge impact. If nothing else, picking up trash and debris in your community is a worthwhile contribution.

Environmental Health

Growing up in my house, as in many African American homes, my mother would spend countless hours cleaning from the kitchen to the bathroom, polishing furniture and washing clothes. One of the traits of her cleaning was the smell of the products she used from lemon fragrance to the strong odor of bleach. She did her best to make sure that our house was clean from top to bottom.

As my brothers and I got older we pitched in and did our share of the household chores, especially on Saturday mornings. Although we cleaned dust and dirt, we never thought about the harsh chemicals we were inhaling in the process.

Household chemicals from cleaning products are some of the most dangerous chemicals to be exposed to and they're usually right under our noses. Detergents, cosmetics, hair care products, bleach, paints, stains, varnishes, dry-cleaned clothes, and garden supplies are a few of a long list of product-causing invisible poisons.

Asthma, which is prevalent in the Black community, has been linked to common cleaning products, as well as other diseases. In fact, most people, especially children, have dozens of pesticides and other toxic compounds in their bodies that are linked to health threats such as cancer and birth defects from everyday consumer products found in the home.

The EPA and the Department of Health and Human Services have labeled some types of phthalates, a common ingredient in many household cleaning products, as a "probable carcinogen"-which means they cause cancer in animals and may cause cancer in humans. The following is a list of common ingredients in cleaners and the possible dangers they cause;

Ammonia: Fatal if swallowed; skin, lung, throat irritant; can cause blindness

Butyl: Irritation and tissue damage from inhalation

Formaldehyde: Known carcinogen

Hydrochloric Acid: Fatal if swallowed; concentrated fumes harmful

Naphtha: Depresses the central nervous system

Perchloroethylene: Damages liver, kidney, nervous system

Petroleum Distillates: Highly flammable; can damage lung tissue and nerve cells

Phenols: Dangerous and suspected carcinogen

Propylene Glycol: Ingestion can damage kidneys, lungs, heart and nervous system

Sodium Hydroxide: Highly caustic. Contact can cause severe damage to eyes, skin, mouth and throat; liver and kidney damage

Sodium Hypochlorite (chlorine bleach): Contact can cause severe damage to eyes, skin, mouth and throat; can cause liver and kidney damage; causes more poisoning exposures than any household chemical

Sulfuric Acid: Can burn skin. Exposure to concentrated fumes can be carcinogenic

Trichloroethane: Damages liver and kidneys

The best tools to use for cleaning your home are all natural products. You can create a mixture of lemon juice and water to use as a disinfectant. Hot water, liquid castile soap, vinegar, lemon and orange essential oils, tea tree oils and baking soda are also good to use for household cleaning.

There are also a number of natural cleaning products that are sold in health food stores across the country. They can easily replace products for laundry and dish detergents, furniture polish, window cleanser, counter tops, shower, and tub and toilet cleaners. It is a far healthier alternative and creates a safer environment to live in.

<u>Citrus Floor Cleaner</u>

1 gallon hot water

2 tablespoons liquid castile soap

15 drops sweet orange essential oil

¼ cup lemon juice

Combine ingredients in a large mop bucket

(Source: Karyn Siegel-Maier; The Naturally Clean Home, Storey Publishing, 1999)

<u>Window Cleaner</u>

3 cups water

¼ cup white vinegar

1 tablespoon lemon juice

Mix and spray

<u>Sink and Toilet Cleaner</u>

½ cup baking soda

¼ cup white vinegar

10 drops tea tree oil

Mix and scrub with brush

The other aspect of cleaning is tidiness. It is important that we clean our homes and dwellings, keeping things in their proper place and order, discarding what we no longer need because in a sense it reflects what goes on

in our lives. When things are neat and orderly for
simple use and functionality it symbolizes peace,
stability, discipline and organization. The opposite, such
as disorganization and clutter reflects chaos and
confusion. Let us create and maintain order in our lives.

<u>**The 42 laws of Maat**</u>

In ancient Egypt, the laws of Maat or the "Declarations of Innocence" were established as a statement for the decease to recite at the time of 'judgment'. The laws were the standard by which a person should live and a measurement of their deeds at the time of death.

Here are the laws as listed by Tony Browder in <u>Nile Valley Contributions to Civilization</u>;

1. I have not done iniquity.
2. I have not robbed with violence.
3. I have not stolen.
4. I have done no murder; I have done no harm.
5. I have not defrauded offerings.
6. I have not diminished obligations.
7. I have not plundered the Netcher.
8. I have not spoken lies.
9. I have not snatched away food.
10. I have not caused pain.
11. I have not committed fornication.
12. I have not caused shedding of tears.
13. I have not dealt deceitfully.
14. I have not transgressed.
15. I have not acted guilefully.
16. I have not laid waste the ploughed land.
17. I have not been an eavesdropper.
18. I have not set my lips in motion against any man.

19. I have not been angry and wrathful except for a just cause.
20. I have not defiled the wife of any man.
21. I have not defiled the wife of any man (repeated twice).
22. I have not polluted myself.
23. I have not caused terror.
24. I have not transgressed (repeated twice).
25. I have not burned with rage.
26. I have not stopped my ears against the words of Right and Truth (Maat).
27. I have not worked grief.
28. I have not acted with insolence.
29. I have not stirred up strife.
30. I have not judged hastily.
31. I have not been an eavesdropper (repeated twice).
32. I have not multiplied words exceedingly.
33. I have not done neither harm nor ill.
34. I have never cursed the king.
35. I have never fouled the water.
36. I have not spoken scornfully.
37. I have never cursed the Netcherw.
38. I have not stolen.
39. I have not defrauded the offerings of the Netcherw.
40. I have not plundered the offerings to the blessed dead.

41. I have not filched the food of the infant, neither have I sinned against the Netcher of my native town.

42. I have not slaughtered with evil intent the cattle of the Netcher.

"Back in the 60s our brothers and sisters were hanged,
how could you gang bang?
I never ever ran from the Ku Klux Klan
and I shouldn't have to run from a black man,
cause that's *Self Destruction*"!...

-Kool Moe Dee verse in *"Self Destruction"*

The Basics of Education

Over the last 60 years there have been numerous attempts to explain the ongoing and pervasive achievement gaps between black and white students across the country. Arguments have ranged from poverty and a lack of proper nutrition, to poor parenting, number of single-parent households, and a high turnover rate of teachers in predominantly black school districts.

Some contemporary white scholars, such as the authors of The Bell Curve, contend that blacks are inherently inferior to whites and are incapable of learning at the same level. Consequently, black children have been disproportionately diagnosed with learning disabilities, prescribed medication such as Ritalin and other derivatives for hyperactivity and short attention spans, held back and placed in special-ed classes. Meanwhile, the elephant in the room has gone largely unnoticed.

The vast majority of the public school education centers on the white experience. Every discipline from history, math and science to geography and social studies is taught from a white perspective. Whether we're talking about Socrates and Greek philosophy, Columbus, Washington, Lincoln or Einstein, white people have given themselves a decidedly advantage by being the hand that controls the pen.

From learning to speak French and Spanish to reciting Shakespeare, the white experience is not only dominant but inescapable. Some people erroneously assume that math is a neutral subject because it deals with numbers, equations, shapes, sizes and measurements but what is counting in Roman numerals? What are the Pythagorean Theorem, and the Newton's method, and who is Euclid and Galileo? Without a doubt, white America tailored each subject to meet their needs and objectives.

As Dr. Carter G. Woodson stated in *The Mis-Education of the Negro* "When you control a man's thinking you do not have to worry about his actions. You do not have to tell him not to stand here or go yonder. He will find his proper place and stay in it. You do not need to send him to the back door. He will go without being told. In fact, if there is no back door, he will cut one for his special benefit. His education makes it necessary".

To further illustrate my point, let's look at a comparative analysis of Supreme Court Justice Clarence Thomas and the late Civil Rights leader Malcolm X:

Clarence Thomas graduated with a law degree from Yale University	Malcolm X dropped out of junior high school and learned an African-centered education behind the walls of a prison

Clarence Thomas is a registered republican, a political party affiliated with right wing, conservative views	Malcolm X founded the OAAU, the Organization of Afro American Unity
Clarence Thomas expressed a desire to rein in Affirmative Action laws and to overhaul a section of the Civil Rights Act	Malcolm X advocated in taking the civil rights struggle of blacks in America to the United Nations to have it recognized in a broader context of human rights to elicit international support
In light of a limited interest in race, Clarence Thomas was unsurprisingly silent regarding Yale's undergraduate residence college named in honor of white supremacist John C. Calhoun	Malcolm X stated "America's greatest crime against the black man was not slavery or lynching, but that he was taught to wear a mask of self-hate and self-doubt".

This is the fundamental difference between training and education. To train someone is to influence their behavior and develop their interest which is usually to the benefit of the trainer. However, to be educated is to be empowered with the ability to think and do for yourself. Clarence Thomas has been "professionally trained" while Malcolm X was actually educated.

Key information to a correct education:

- Africans in ancient Egypt were the founding fathers and mothers of civilization, creating dynasties that spanned over thousands of years that included temples, monuments and pyramids. They were the first of the Pharaohs in recorded history.
- One of the earliest discoveries of math was the "Ishango Bone" found in Zaire.
- In Ethiopia, Africans created the first known system of government.
- The first evidence of cognitive thought in humans was discovered in a cave on the tip of South Africa. It was a pattern of diamonds on a piece of art that dates back to 77,000 years ago.
- Some of the sharpest cutting edges used in Australia before the arrival of the Europeans were made from natural glass and were flaked with amazing symmetry by the Aboriginals. In addition, a network of fish-traps and systems of weirs have been found and recorded by archaeologists. These walls, traps and races

were erected to artificially connect lakes and swamps and portion off segments of seas to capture eels, fish and shell fish and were used for hundreds of years.

- Africans were one of the first peoples to build boats and were sailing to America trading with the indigenous people for more than two thousand years before Columbus was born. Evidence unearthed in Mexico reveal gigantic Olmec Heads of African faces carved out of stone, some of which stand over 8 feet high, 18 feet in circumference, weighing between 10 and 40 tons and are over 3,000 years old.
- Imhotep, who designed the step pyramid at Saqqara, is the first multi-genius in recorded history.
- In Zimbabwe, Africans built a great city out of stone with granite so accurately carved that they were fitted together without the use of cement that dates back to the 11th century.
- The Dogon people of Mali were studying the solar system with accuracy and precision with the naked eye for more than a thousand years before the invention of the telescope.
- In Tanzania, Africans built 13 iron furnaces and were producing carbon steel over 2,000 years ago.
- Scientist discovered a common gene in all races of people that traces back to an African woman, the common ancestor of all humans.

- A 2,000 year old glider was uncovered in Egypt proving that Africans had advance knowledge of physics and aeronautics.

- The Aboriginal peoples of Australia who migrated from the African continent several thousand years ago developed technology that involved a complex understanding of the many sciences and processes. An understanding of the laws of physics and the complexities of aerodynamics enabled the skilled creation of the boomerang, the spear, the woomera and the bull roarer. A deep understanding of biology and chemistry enabled Aboriginal people to select foods from nature at the correct times and to use complex processes to extract toxins from plants and animals.

- Africans created the first calendar in 10,000 B.C.E. determining a year as 365 and ¼ days

- The famous university of Djenne, rebuilt as the University of Sankore was founded in the fourteenth century in Timbuktu, Mali. The university attracted students from within Africa and from countries outside the continent to include Europe and Asia. As a center of scholarship, the institute taught the subjects of philosophy, literature, history, medicine, law and advanced courses of mathematics to include algebra and trigonometry.

- The Dufuna Canoe was discovered near the region of the River Yobe in Nigeria by a Fulani heardsman in May 1987. The canoe's almost black wood is an organic material of African mahogany. Several Radio-Carbon tests conducted in laboratories of Universities in Europe and America indicate that the canoe is over 8,000 years old, thus making it the oldest in Africa and 3rd oldest in the world. Peter Breunig of the University of Frankfort, Germany, an archeologist, says the canoe's age "forces a reconsideration of Africa's role in the history of water transport." According to Breunig "The bow and stern are both carefully worked to points, giving the boat a notably more elegant form", compared to the dugout made of conifer wood from Pesse in the Netherlands, whose blunt ends and thick sides seem crude". To go by its stylistic sophistication, he reasons, "it is highly probable that the Dufuna boat does not represent the beginning of a tradition, but has already undergone a long development, and that the origins of water transport in Africa lie even further back in time."

- The nail which is the main tool necessary for carpentry and construction was invented and used in ancient Egypt as early as 3,400 B.C.
- "Reed Paper", the name given to the first form of paper ever used was developed as woven papyrus in ancient Kemet during the fourth century B.C.

- In hillside caves of southwest Germany, archeologists uncovered the beginnings of music and art by early modern humans migrating into Europe from Africa. The "Bone Flute" is the earliest known instrument in the world and is made out of bird bone and mammoth ivory. Designed with a pattern of holes to orchestrate sounds, it has been radiocarbon dated as 43,000 years old.

- Medu Netcher, also known as known as hieroglyphics, is the earliest known alphabet in recorded history. The writing first appeared in Egypt's Sinai desert at a site called Wadi Ameyra, approximately 3,000 B.C. The wall carvings also reveal the reign of one of Kemet's earliest queens, Neith-Hotep, who ruled 5,000 years ago as regent to the Pharaoh Djer.

<u>Essential personalities;</u>

Stephen Bantu Biko - prominent anti-apartheid activist in South Africa

Haile Gerima-filmmaker extraordinaire, creator of Sankofa

Huey P. Newton and Bobby Seale –activists, founders of the Black Panther Party

Margaret Walker Alexander- master poet and educator

Louis Armstrong- Jazz legend, musical innovator

Chinua Achebe – author of "Things Fall Apart"

Public Enemy- revolutionary musical activists

Muhammad Ali- Boxing icon and social activist

James Baldwin- Civil Rights activist

Count Basie-Music innovator and jazz master

Mary McLeod Bethune- Civil Rights Leader and educator

Julian Bond-Civil Rights Leader, prominent NAACP personality

Stokely Carmichael- powerful leader of the SNCC

Ossie Davis-legendary actor, writer and director

W.E.B. Dubois- prominent scholar, co-founder of the NAACP

Kool Moe Dee-rap music legend and lyrical genius

Earl Graves, Sr. - publisher of Black Enterprise magazine

Colin Powell- awarded the Presidential Medal of Freedom

Ida B. Wells- President of the Anti-Lynching League

Oprah Winfrey- Entrepreneur extraordinaire, entertainment mogul

Andrew Young- US Ambassador to the United Nations

Frederick Douglass-abolitionist, entrepreneur, freedom fighter

Queen Hatshepsut- warrior and powerful ruler of ancient Egypt

KRS One-Hip Hop revolutionist and visionary

Malcolm X-Civil Rights Leader, revolutionary activist

Hannibal- legendary military leader and strategist

Kwame Nkrumah- colonial liberator, President of Ghana

Nelson Mandela- freedom fighter, President and legendary leader of South Africa

Imhotep-father of medicine, first multi-genius (physician, sage, scribe)

Ramses-notable ruler of ancient Egypt

Toussaint L'Ouverture- warrior, leader and revolutionary icon

Honorable Elijah Muhammad- founder and leader of the Nation of Islam

Nzinga- great warrior Queen of Angola

Barack Obama- most accomplished President in the history of the United States

Grandmaster Mele Mel- rap music pioneer, one of the world's leading poets

Marcus Garvey- legendary freedom fighter, visionary, leader and activist

Quincy Jones-multi-musical genius (musician, composer, arranger, producer)

Listervelt Middleton- poet, innovator, grass roots activist

Bob Marley-reggae icon, creative genius

Booker T. Washington- educator, founder of Tuskegee Institute

Patrick Lumumba-powerful speaker and advocate for African liberation and development

Otis Redding-rhythm and blues legend and voice of a generation

Mansa Musa-emperor of the West African empire of Mali

Louis Armstrong- musical trailblazer and jazz legend

Gladys Knight- soulful queen and all-time music legend

Dorothy Height-Human Rights crusader and Civil Rights icon

X-Clan- militant and cultural voice of hip hop

Dr. Leonard Jeffries- powerful scholar and leader of the freedom movement

Scholars, Historians, and their notable works;

- Chiekh Anta Diop-*The African Origins of Civilization*

- Maulana Karenga- *Kwanzaa: A Celebration of Family, Community and Culture*

- John Henrik Clarke-*Critical Lessons in Slavery and the Slave Trade*

- John G. Jackson- *Introduction To African Civilizations*

- Anthony T. Browder- *Nile Valley Contributions to Civilization*

- Llaila Africa- *African Holistic Health*

- Na'im Akbar-*Know Thy Self*

- Marimba Ani- *Yurugu*

- Molefi Kete Asante-*Afrocentricity*

- Yosef Ben-Jochannan- *African Origins of the Major Western Religions*

- George GM James- *Stolen Legacy: Greek Philosophy Is Stolen Egyptian Philosophy*

- Runoko Rashidi- *African Presence in Early Asia*

- Ivan Van Sertima- *They Came Before Columbus: The African Presence in Ancient America*

- Chancellor Williams- *The Destruction of Black Civilization*

- Amos Wilson- *Black On Black Violence*

- Francis Cress Welsing- *The Isis Papers*

- Indus Khamit Kush- *What They Never Told You in History Class*

- Carter G. Woodson-*The Mis-Education of the Negro*

- Asa Hilliard- *SBA: The Reawakening Of The African Mind*

- John Hope Franklin- *From Slavery To Freedom*

- Wade W. Nobles- *Seeking the Sakhu: Foundational Writings for an African Psychology*

- Frantz Fanon- *Black Skin, White Masks*

- Na'im Akbar- *Chains and Images of Psychological Slavery*

- Charles Finch- *The African Background To Medical Science*

- Walter Rodney- *How Europe Underdeveloped Africa*

Holidays, Celebrations and the Green Shirt Event

Many religions are associated with certain holidays, celebrations and ceremonies. Jews celebrate Rosh Hashanah, the Jewish New Year and Yom Kippur, their holy day of atonement. Christians celebrate Christmas, the birth of Christ, New Years and Easter, a celebration of Christ's resurrection.

Muslims participate in Ramadan, a month of fasting which is followed with the festival celebration of Eid Al-Fitr. For Americans, one of the most popular holidays of the year is Thanksgiving, a non-religious gathering of family and friends.

From our history of yam festivals, we recognize the tradition of African people coming together in celebration. We are reminded of our ancestors and their celebrations of in-gatherings across the continent from Egypt and Nubia to Ashanti-land, and Yoruba-land among several other regions. Therefore, in an effort to come together with family and friends we are encouraged to do so as it reflects a customary practice of communal engagement.

Therefore, we acknowledge and celebrate the African-centered spiritual practice "Seven" with an annual commemoration day on the last Saturday of April as the "Green Shirt" event. Subsequently, we reconvene on the last Saturday of October, the complimentary date of the year, to represent the balance and duality of life, i.e.

male/female, right/left, up/down, back/front, sun/moon, day/night, fire/water, etc.

Seven is represented by two candles in the colors of gold and green. Green symbolizes Africa, the "Motherland", not only the birth place of African people but the human family as well. The color signifies the land of our ancestors, their triumphs and struggles, hopes, dreams and aspirations, and the legacy as well as the challenges they left behind for future generations.

Gold represents the value of our commitment in struggle and our service to the Creator. It illustrates what it means to stand for truth, justice, righteousness, peace, harmony and reciprocity. It also reflects our individual and collective will and determination and obligation to ourselves, community and nation.

The bi-annual Green Shirt event is a wellness party where we encourage wearing a green shirt to the event. It begins with lighting the two candles and pouring libation in honor of our ancestors, in recognition and remembrance.

Libation is followed with a group walk through our communities for the benefit of exercise. Upon return, we gather for a "potluck" of healthy and natural food and drink, and conclude with a group discussion of substantive dialog, book exchange, and encouragement until we meet again.

We are also encouraged to celebrate Kwanzaa each year with a week of activities beginning December 26th thru January 1st. The Nguzo Saba, the seven principals of Kwanzaa, allows us to reaffirm our commitment and vision as a people.

The principals are (Swahili and English interpretation and meaning):

1. Umoja (Unity) - to strive for and maintain unity in the family, community, nation and race.

2. Kujichagulia (Self-Determination)-to define ourselves, name ourselves, create for ourselves and speak for ourselves.

3. Ujima (Collective Work and Responsibility)-to build and maintain our community together and make our brother's and sister's problems our problems and to solve them together.

4. Ujamaa (Cooperative Economics)-to build and maintain our own stores, shops and other businesses and to profit from them together.

5. Nia (Purpose) - to make our collective vocation the building and developing of our community in order to restore our people to their traditional greatness.

6. Kuumba (Creativity)-to do always as much as
    we can, in the way we can, in order to leave our
    community more beautiful and beneficial than
    we inherited it.

7. Imani (Faith)-to believe with all of our heart in
    our people, our parents, our teachers, our
    leaders and the righteousness and victory of our
    struggle.

<u>Songs of Vibranium (Faith and Freedom)</u>

Marvin Gaye- What's Going On?

Denise Williams – Black Butterfly

Temptations- Ball of Confusion

Caron Wheeler- Livin' in the Light

James Brown – Say it Loud (I'm Black and I'm Proud)

Soul II Soul featuring Caron Wheeler – Keep on Movin'

Isley Jasper Isley - Caravan of Love

James Weldon Johnson- Lift Every Voice and Sing

McFadden and Whitehead- Ain't No Stopping Us Now

Gil Scott-Heron- The Revolution Will Not Be Televised

Teddy Pendergrass – Happy Kwanzaa

Grandmaster Flash and the Furious Five- The Message

Bob Marley – Get Up Stand Up

Curtis Mayfield – We Got to Have Peace

Angie Stone – Brotha

Michael Jackson- Heal the World

Brian McKnight – Win

The Isley Brothers- Harvest for the World

Kool Moe Dee featuring KRS One and Chuck D- Rise N Shine

Michael Jackson – Man in the Mirror

Louis Armstrong w/ Kenny G – What a Wonderful World

Mariah Carey featuring Whitney Houston – When You Believe

Billie Holiday- Strange Fruit

R. Kelly – I Believe I Can Fly

Erykah Badu – On & On

Indie Arie- Strength Courage & Wisdom

Grandmaster Melle Mel – Beat Street Breakdown

Yolanda Adams – Never Give Up

Sam Cooke - A Change Is Gonna Come

Jay Z, Rihanna, Bono and the Edge – Stranded (Haiti Mon Amour)

R. Kelly – Sign of a Victory

Ruben Studdard – Flying Without Wings

Grandmaster Flash and the Furious Five - The King

Marvin Gaye – Mercy Mercy Me

James Brown – I Don't Want Nobody to Give Me Nothing

King Dream Chorus and Holiday Crew – King Holiday

Harold Melvin and the Blue Notes – Wake Up Everybody

Sounds of Blackness – Optimistic

Peter Tosh - African

Public Enemy – Fight the Power

Earth, Wind and Fire - That's the Way of the World

Bill Withers- Lean On Me

Pointer Sisters – Yes We Can-Can

Sounds of Blackness – Hold On (A Change Is Coming)

KRS One- You Must Learn

Tevin Campbell & Quincy Jones- Tomorrow (A Better You, Better Me)

Edwin Starr-War (What Is It Good For?)

Stevie Wonder- Living For The City

John Legend featuring The Roots- Shine

Arrested Development- Mr. Wendal

In Spirit of Sankofa

The movie Sankofa is monumental to the African and African American experience. First, the name itself is Akan and means "one must return to the past in order to move forward." The story is about a modern day African American woman who is sent on a spiritual journey in time to experience the pain and suffering of slavery and the ultimate discovery of her African identity.

A spirit that is equally reflected in the heroic and defiant acts of Harriet Tubman, Sojourner Truth, Frederick Douglass, Nat Turner, Denmark Vesey and all of our known and unknown ancestors who were some of the most courageous human beings to ever walk on earth! This is the spirit of Wakanda!

<u>**Conclusion**</u>

The purpose of creating a dialog is to engage in the
issues that impact the lives of people of African descent
and the communities in which we live. This is
accomplished by addressing the challenges imposed by
society based on race and the effects of culture. It is
equally intended to raise awareness regarding our
health and self-development. Finally, it is a challenge
for African people to strive to be the best that we can
be, and to restore our pride and dignity so that we can
sit down at the table of humanity and not be the
servants. We must rise and overcome our obstacles
and prepare for the sun to shine on a new day in African
history.

About the Author

Sean XLG Mitchell is a hip hop activist, historian and former rap artist. In 1990, he became the first rapper to win a national music competition on Lee Bailey's syndicated program *Radioscope*. In 1993, his musical talents helped to pass Washington, DC's Initiative 37, the Nuclear Weapons Disarmament Act. As an artist, he released underground hits, most notably "Money Makes the World Go Around" and has worked extensively in the African American community for many years.

He began organizing and leading community based study groups, volunteering at the Roots Activity Learning Center in Washington, DC, served as a youth mentor at Aberdeen Proving Grounds, and has advocated for funding and services to assist individuals with developmental disabilities.

Sean is the creator of the African American spiritual practice *Seven* and author of *Introduction to Ka-Maat, Hip Hop Hooray: Celebrating 30 Years of Rap Music* and co-author of *The Million Dollar Hip Hop Challenge* with Kool Rock of the Fat Boys. He is a devoted husband and father and lives in metropolitan Washington, DC.